THE TEACHINGS

PTA

The Oldest Book in the World

First published Circa 2388 B.C.
Fifth Kemetic (Egyptian) Dynasty
under the title:

Teachings of the Prefect of the City, Dja Ptahhotep
under the majesty of the king of the South and the North,
Assa Djed-Ka-Ra, living eternally forever.

Asa G. Hilliard III, Larry Williams
and Nia Damali
Editors

Illustrated by Babatunde K.S. Abdullah

© Copyright, 1987

This book is dedicated to the numerous African Scribes who labored for generations to instill in African peoples the ancient Kemetic teaching of the Mysteries, "Man, Know Thyself."

ACKNOWLEDGMENTS

Special acknowledgments are due to the following persons whose efforts made The Teachings Of Ptahhotep: The Oldest Book In The World a reality. Special thanks to Faye Bellamy for transcribing dictations of the manuscript for The Teachings Of Ptahhotep into written form. John W. Gunn, Jr. for type-setting the manuscript for publication. Babatunde K.S. Abdullah for the cover design and illustration.

TABLE OF CONTENTS

INTRODUCTION

A man with wisdom is better off than a stupid man with any amount of charm and superstition.

African Proverb

Sometime during the early 1800's, across the Hapi (Nile) river from Waset ("Luxor" to the Arabs and "Thebes" to the Greeks), on the west bank in the "Valley of the Kings," in the eleventh dynasty tomb of one of the Intef Pharaohs, a precious papyrus was found. The cemetery at the time of the find was called Drah-abu'l-Neggah, by its Arab name. The find was eighteen pages of papyrus on which near perfect hieratic writing was found, writing closest to the Mdw Ntr (hieroglyphic). As is well known, many Kemetic written and architectural forms are much more pure the older they are. This also appears to be true of their ideas, virtues or moral principals.

Monsieur E. Prisse d'Avennes, who was responsible for the excavations, gave the papyrus to the Biblioteque Nationale in Paris. He published the papyrus in 1847 in Paris.

This papyrus contained two writings, the first being incomplete. The first document was the last part of the Teachings addressed by an unknown scribe to Kagame, a scribe who is said to have composed his work at the beginning of the reign of Seneferu, (2575 B.C. - 2551 B.C.) founder of the Fourth Dynasty, builder of the Great Pyramid at Giza. Most of the contents of the Teachings to Kagame are lost or destroyed. Otherwise, it would be the oldest complete book in human history.

The second and longest (14 pages) part of the papyrus, sometimes called the Book of Ptahhotep and sometimes called the Prisse Papyrus, contains a complete work of Ptahhotep. Two other papyri, one from the Middle Kingdom and one from the New Kingdom, and one wooden tablet from the New Kingdom also survived. The other two papyri were given to the British Museum. The wooden tablet was given to the Cairo Museum. It was an incomplete rendering.

There is a tomb for Ptahhotep near the Step Pyramid in the cemetery at Sakkara. Many authorities believe, and the strongest evidence supports the belief, that he was the Ptahhotep who was the author of the book. The papyrus document says that the author lived during the reign of Menkauhor (2396 B.C. - 2388 B.C.) and Assa Djed-Ka-Ra (2388 B.C. - 2356 B.C.). The papyrus referred to Ptahhotep as the favored one of Assa, Ptahhotep was his grand uncle and also his tutor. Ptahhotep himself was said to be the eldest legitimate son of an unnamed Pharaoh, and was 110 years old when he wrote his book. M. Revilout has said that Ptahhotep was in line to become Pharaoh, but that he renounced the throne and politics in favor of the priestly calling. This is consistent with the description of Kemetic education as providing for a choice of two paths in higher education, one more sacred and one more secular, such as in politics.

By 3100 B.C. ancient Kmt (called Egypt by the Greeks) had become a nation state. The only clear records of an older nation state were further south in Ta-Seti, in Nubia. Abundant carvings, skeletal remains, architectural remains and even well preserved bodies provide unmistakable evidence of the development from the south of ancient Africa's earliest classical civilization. Another source of information about both Ta-Seti and Kmt is the Mdw Ntr (sometimes called Mdw (word) Netcher (God), or Word of the Gods, or simply Holy Writing (thousands of years later the Greeks would call these writings hieroglyphics.

Mdw Netcher is Africa's and the world's oldest recorded writing system. What is important about the Mdw Netcher is that there is no evidence of a developmental period. This writing system simply appears fully developed as it must have existed ages before either Kmt or Ta-Seti came into being. The existence of this writing alone is testimonial to the development of early civilization in the ancient Hapi (Nile) Valley. In other words, what we refer to today as "civilization" existed in the Hapi Valley even earlier than evidence for the establishment of the world's first two nation states. We must remember that the Mdw Netcher is not the only evidence of pre-Kemetic national civilization farther South in the

Hapi Valley. The burial of the dead, the existence of a highly developed monotheistic religious system, the existence of a pharoanic led political system, the existence of a highly developed science of astronomy and many other things associated with cooperative and intelligent human society proved the existence of early civilization in the Hapi Valley, more developed than anywhere else in the world at that time.

In light of the history of colonization, slavery, segregation and racism in the world, and especially in light of the effects of these things on the colonization of information, it is important that we be explicit about the fact that this ancient Kemetic and pre-Kemetic civilization was native African. That means that it was a black or Africoid civilization. If one places the evidence from skeletal remains, mummified remains, carvings, paintings and ancient historical accounts into chronological order, the blackness of ancient Kmt, ancient Ta-Seti and even more ancient Hapi (Nile) Valley cultures will be obvious to any observer.

The colonization of Africa, the enslavement of African people, and the segregation of Africans in the African Diaspora was accompanied by a wholesale, systematic falsification of the human record. It left the descendants of Africans and others throughout the world in almost total darkness, regarding the contributions of

African people to the population of the world and to world civilization.

An active effort on a fairly large scale is now underway to recover and to reconstitute the lost, stolen, suppressed and distorted history of Africa's people in the world. There have been many scholars such as Edward Wilmot Blyden, Martin Delaney, the honorable Marcus Mosiah Garvey, W.E.B. DuBois, Carter G. Woodson, Cheikh Anta Diop, Chancellor Williams, Yosef Ben Jochannan, John G. Jackson, John Henrik Clarke and a host of other courageous African scholars who have worked to set the record straight. In their wake they have left as a legacy a new army of researchers who are even more determined to see that the fruits of the labor of these giants will be harvested in our lifetime. It is toward that end that a re-presentation of the ancient records in all their forms is absolutely essential. It is essential that they be made available to the widest possible audience. Audiences that until now have been treated with excerpts and interpretations or translations in archaic language.

Many of us who work in this field have a deep and abiding faith in the wisdom of the masses of our people, feeling certain that wisdom may be fed by the re-presentation of African information and documentation that has, until now, remained well beyond the reach of our people. It is toward that goal and in this spirit that this presentation is offered. In doing so we freely acknowledge the model and leadership provided by Dr. Maulana Karenga and his development of Ancient African sacred texts, The Husia. It was the first attempt to make the wisdom of ancient Africa accessible to the masses of our people.

The earliest Mdw Netcher writings described Offering lists to the deity or to its manifestations and powers. Later prayers of offerings were substituted for the Offering list. These writings as with almost all writings in ancient Kmt emerged out of a profound religious orientation toward the world. This religious orientation found its expression in preparations for life after death or for the resurrection. However, lost to many analysts is the fact that in the preparation for life after death or for the resurrection, the supplicant was actually articulating a set of values and a code of behaviors by which to live one's life in the world before death. No higher human behavioral code has been found anywhere in human history than the earliest code of the ancient Kamites.

Following the lists of offerings and prayers, another form of writing appeared in the early dynastic period in Kmt. In the temples and tombs prepared for deceased persons, we find that there was concern that the deceased be able to say, on Judgement Day, that he or she had followed God's will. Therefore, there emerged in the old kingdom the practice of writing down declarations of virtues. These declarations of virtues appear in the new kingdom, the 18th Dynastic Period, as the "Negative Confessions." In popular form there were 42 of these "Negative Confessions" or the "Declarations of Virtues." According to Biblical history, Moses was an Egyptian priest who was learned in all the wisdom of Egypt, a wisdom literature that included the Per-em-Hru (the Book of Coming Forth From Darkness Into Light) or as it is popularly called, "The Book of the Dead." Forty-two "Negative Confessions" or "Declarations of Virtues" are found in this book, and bear a striking resemblance to the much shorter list of virtues which are stated as "Commandments" in the Old Testament.

It is the next form of literature to emerge that we present here. Some writers have referred to it as the Wisdom Literature of the ancient Kamites, instructions in wisdom, or as the ancient Kamites themselves called it, simply "Instructions.

The earliest incomplete instruction text that survives are the instructions to Kagame, a vizier who served both Huni and Seneferu of the Third and Fourth Dynasties respectively. This is followed by the instructions of Hardjedef, the prince, for his son Auibre. Hardjedef was the son of Khufu of the 4th Dynasty, and grandson of Seneferu. However, these instructions are very short and are incomplete. So the oldest complete set of instructions is the 37 Teachings or <u>Instructions of Ptahhotep</u>. This makes the <u>Instructions of Ptahhotep</u> the oldest textbook in the world.

The <u>Instructions of Ptahhotep</u> were copied during the Middle Kingdom on papyri that are still preserved. Some Egyptologists believed that because the instructions were attributed to Ptahhotep and because there was indeed an old kingdom sage by that name, and because Middle Kingdom writers attributed the sayings to that sage, who is said to have served under King Assa of the 5th Dynasty, therefore they should accept that attribution in the absence of compelling evidence to the contrary. Even if it were Middle Kingdom material at an age (12th Dynasty) of approximately 2,000 B.C. it would still be the oldest wisdom literature in the world. Given a 5th Dynastic Age, we can say that the Instructions of Ptahhotep belong to a period approximately 2,500 years before Christ.

It is with great pleasure that these profound instructions are once again made available to African people and to the world. It was wisdom such as this that made people throughout the world come to Kmt, to Africa, to drink at the fountainhead of wisdom. This is true of students from Asia including the Hebrews and later the greatest classical scholars of the Greeks and the Romans.

The reader is referred to several translations of the book of Ptahhotep in the selected bibliography. We have consolidated in this edited version the best translations in modern rather than archaic English.

THE TEACHINGS
OF
PTAHHOTEP
The Oldest Book in the World

These are instructions by the Mayor of the City who is also the Vizier. His name is Ptahhotep and he serves under Pharoah Assa who lives for all eternity. The Mayor of the City, Vizier Ptahhotep, addressed the Supreme Divinity, the Deity as follows:

"God upon the two crocodiles." (Reference to Heru) who is sometimes shown standing on two crocodiles. My God, the process of aging brings senility. My mind decays and forgetfulness of the things of yesterday has already begun. Feebleness has come and weakness grows. Childlike one sleeps all day. The eyes are dim and the ears are becoming deaf. The strength is being sapped. The mouth has grown silent and does not speak. The bones ache through and through. Good things now seem evil. The taste is gone. What old age does to people in evil is every thing. The nose is clogged and does not breath. It is painful even to stand or to sit. May your servant be authorized to use the status that old age affords, to teach the hearers, so as to tell them the words of those who have listened to the ways of our ancestors, and of those who have listened to the Gods. May I do this for you, so that strife may be banned from among our people, and so that the Two Shores may serve you?

Then the majesty of the Deity said to

Ptahhotep, go ahead and instruct him in the Ancient Wisdom. May he become a model for the children of the great. May obedience enter into him, and may he be devoted to the one who speaks to him. No one is born wise.

And so begins the formulation of Mdw Nfr, *good speech*, to be spoken by the Prince, the Count, God's beloved, the eldest son of the Pharoah, the son of his body, Mayor of the City and Vizier, Ptahhotep, instructs the ignorant in the knowledge and in the standards of *good speech*. It will profit those who hear. It will be a loss to those who transgress. Ptahhotep began to speak to "Pharaoh's son" (to posterity).

1. Do not be proud and arrogant with your knowledge. Consult and converse with the ignorant and the wise, for the limits of art are not reached. No artist ever possesses that perfection to which he should aspire. *Good speech* is more hidden than green-stone (emeralds), yet it may be found among maids at the grindstones.

2. If you meet a disputant in the heat of action, one who is more powerful than you, simply fold your arms and bend your back. To confront him will not make him agree with you. Pay no attention to his *evil*

speech. If you do not confront him while he is raging, people will call him an ignoramus. Your self-control will be the match for his evil utterances.

3. If you meet a disputant in action, one who is your equal, one who is on your level, you will overcome him by being silent while he is speaking evilly. There will be much talk among those who hear and your name will be held in high regard among the great.

4. If you meet a disputant in action who is a poor man and who is not your equal do not attack him because he is weak. Leave him alone. He will confound himself. Do not answer him just so that you can relieve your own heart. Do not vent yourself against your opponent. Wretched is he who injures a poor man. If you ignore him listeners will wish to do what your want. You will beat him through their reproof.

5. If you are a man who leads, a man who controls the affairs of many, then seek the most perfect way of performing your responsibility so that your conduct will be blameless. Great is Maat (truth, justice

and righteousness). It is everlasting. Maat has been unchanged since the time of Asar. To create obstacles to the following of laws, is to open a way to a condition of violence. The transgressor of laws is punished, although the greedy person overlooks this. Baseness may obtain riches, yet crime never lands its wares on the shore. In the end only Maat lasts. Man says, "Maat is my father's ground."

6. Do not scheme against people. God will punish accordingly; If a man says, "I shall live by scheming," he will lack bread for his mouth. If a man says, "I will be rich," he will have to say, "My cleverness has trapped me." If he says, "I will trap for myself" he will not be able to say, "I trapped for my profit." If a man says, "I will rob someone," he will end by being given to a stranger. People's schemes do not prevail. God's command is what prevails. Therefore, live in the midst of peace. What God gives comes by itself.

7. If you are one among guests at the table of a person who is more powerful than you, take what that person gives just as it is set before you. Look at what is before you.

Don't stare at your host. Don't speak to him until he asks. One does not know what may displease him. Speak when he has spoken to you. Then your words will please the heart. The man who has plenty of the means of existence acts as his Ka commands. He will give food to those who he favors. It is the Ka that makes his hand stretch out. The great man gibes to the chosen man, thus eating is under the direction of God. It is a fool who complains about it.

8. If your are a person of trust sent by one great person to another great person, be careful to stick to the essence of the message that you were asked to transmit. Give the message exactly as he gave it to you. Guard against provocative speech which makes one great person angry with another. Just keep to the truth. Do not exceed it. However, even though there may have been an out-burst in the message you should not repeat it. Do not malign anyone, great or small, the Ka abhors it.

9. If you plow and if there is growth in your field and God lets it prosper in your hand, don't boast to your neighbor. One has

great respect for the silent person. A person of character is a person of wealth. If that person robs, he or she is like a crocodile in the middle of the waters. If God gives you children, don't impose on one who has no children. Neither should you decry or brag about having your own children, for there is many a father who has grief and many a mother with children who is less content than another. It is the lonely whom God nurtures while the family man prays for a follower.

10. If you are poor, then serve a person of worth so that your conduct may be well with God. Do not bring up the fact that he was once poor. Do not be arrogant towards him just because you know about his former state. Respect him now for his position of authority. As for fortune, it obeys its own law and that is her will. It is God's gift. It is God who makes him worthy and who protects him while he sleeps, or who can turn away from him.

11. Follow your heart as long as you live. Do no more than is required. Do not shorten the time of "follow the heart", since that offends the Ka. Don't waste time on daily

cares over and beyond providing for your household. When wealth finally comes, then follow your heart. Wealth does no good if you are glum.

12. If you are a wise man, train up a son who will be pleasing to God. If he is straight and takes after you take good care of him. Do everything that is good for him. He is your son, your Ka begot him. Don't withdraw your heart from him. But an offspring can make trouble. If your son strays and neglects your council and disobeys all that is said, with his mouth spouting evil speech, then punish him for all his talk. God will hate him who crosses you. His guilt was determined in the womb. He who God makes boatless cannot cross the water.

13. If you are a guard in the storehouse, stand or sit rather than leave your post and trespass into someone else's place. Follow this rule from the first. Never leave your post, even when fatigued. Keen is the face to him who enters announced, and spacious is the seat of him who has been asked to come in. The storehouse has fixed rules. All behavior is strictly by the rule.

Only a God can penetrate the secure warehouse where the rules are followed, even by privileged persons.

14. If you are among the people then gain your supporters by building trust. The trusted man is one who does not speak the first thing that comes to mind; and he will become a leader. A man of means has a good name, and his face is benign. People will praise him even without his knowledge. On the other hand, he whose heart obeys his belly asks for contempt of himself in the place of love. His heart is naked. His body is unanointed. The great hearted is a gift of God. He who is ruled by his appetite belongs to the enemy.

15. Report the thing that you were commissioned to report without error. Give your advice in the high council. If you are fluent in your speech, it will not be hard for you to report. Nor will anyone say of you, "who is he to know this?" As to the authorities, their affairs will fail if they punish you for speaking truth. They should be silent upon hearing the report that you have rendered as you have been told.

If you are a man who leads, a man whose authority reaches widely, then you should do perfect things, those which posterity will remember. Don't listen to the words of flatterers or to words that puff you up with pride and vanity.

17. If you are a person who judges, listen carefully to the speech of one who pleads. Don't stop the person from telling you everything that they had planned to tell you. A person in distress wants to pour out his or her heart, even more than they want their case to be won. If you are one who stops a person who is pleading, that person will say "why does he reject my plea?" Of course not all that one pleads for can be granted, but a good hearing soothes the heart. The means for getting a true and clear explanation is to listen with kindness.

18. If you want friendship to endure in the house that you enter, the house of a master, of a brother or of a friend, then in what ever place you enter beware of approaching the women there. Unhappy is the place where this is done. Unwelcome is he who intrudes on them. A thousand men are turned away from their good be-

cause of a short moment that is like a dream, and then that moment is followed by death that comes from having known that dream. Anyone who encourages you to take advantage of the situation gives you poor advice. When you go to do it, your heart says no. If you are one who fails through the lust of women, then no affair of yours can prosper.

19. If you want to have perfect conduct, to be free from every evil, then above all guard against the vice of greed. Greed is a grievous sickness that has no cure. There is no treatment for it. It embroils fathers, mothers and the brothers of the mother. It parts the wife from the husband. Greed is a compound of all the evils. It is a bundle of all hateful things. That person endures whose rule is rightness, who walks a straight line, for that person will leave a legacy by such behavior. On the other hand, the greedy has no tomb.

20. Do not be greedy in the division of things. Do not covet more than your share. Don't be greedy towards your relatives. A mild person has a greater claim than the harsh one. Poor is the person who forgets his

relatives. He is deprived of their company. Even a little bit of what is wanted will turn a quarreler into a friendly person.

21. When you prosper and establish your home, love your wife with ardor. Then fill her belly and clothe her back. Caress her. Give her ointments to soothe her body. Fulfill her wishes for as long as you live. She is a fertile field for her husband. Do not be brutal. Good manners will influence her better than force. Do not contend with her in the courts. Keep her from the need to resort to outside powers. Her eye is her storm when she gazes. It is by such treatment that she will be compelled to stay in your house.

22. Help your friends with things that you have, for you have these things by the grace of God. If you fail to help your friends, one will say you have a selfish Ka. One plans for tomorrow, but you do not know what tomorrow will bring. The right soul is the soul by which one is sustained. If you do praiseworthy deeds your friends will say, "welcome" in your time of need.

Don't repeat slander nor should you even listen to it. It is the spouting of the hot bellied. Just report a thing that has been observed, not something that has been heard secondhand. If it is something negligible, don't even say anything. He who is standing before you will recognize your worth. Slander is like a terrible dream against which one covers the face.

24. If you are a man of worth who sits at the council of a leader, concentrate on being excellent. Your silence is much better than boasting. Speak when you know that you have a solution. It is the skilled person who should speak when in council. Speaking is harder than all other work. The one who understands this makes speech a servant.

25. If you are mighty and powerful then gain respect through knowledge and through your gentleness of speech. Don't order things except as it is fitting. The one who provokes others gets into trouble. Don't be haughty lest you be humbled. But also don't be mute lest you be chided. When you answer one who is fuming, turn your face and control yourself. The flame of the

hot hearted sweeps across every thing. But he who steps gently, his path is a paved road. He who is agitated all day has no happy moments but he who amuses himself all day can't keep his fortune.

26. Do not disturb a great man or distract his attention when he is occupied, trying to understand his task. When he is thus occupied, he strips his body through the love of what he does. Love for the work which they do brings men closer to God. These are the people who succeed in what they do.

27. Teach the great what is useful to them. Be an aide to the great before the people. If you let your knowledge impress your leader, your substenance from him will then come from his soul. As his favorite's belly is filled, so will your back be clothed and his help will be there to sustain you. For your leader whom you love and who lives by useful knowledge, he in turn will give you good support. Thus will the love of you endure in his belly. He is a soul who loves to listen.

28. If you are an official of high standing, and you are commissioned to satisfy the many, then hold to a straight line. When you speak don't lean to one side or to the other. Beware lest someone complain, saying to the judges, "he has distorted things", and then your very deeds will turn into a judgment of you.

29. If you are angered by a misdeed, then lean toward a man on account of his rightness. Pass over the misdeed and don't remember it, since God was silent to you on the first day of your misdeed.

30. If you are great after having been humble, if you have gained your wealth after having been poor, and then go to a town that you know and that knows your former condition, don't put your trust in your newly acquired wealth which has come to you as a gift of God. If you do, one day someone there who is poor may very well overtake you.

31. Accept the authority of your leaders then your house will endure in its wealth. Your rewards will come from the right place. Wretched is he who opposes his leader.

One lives as long as he is mild. Baring your arm does not hurt it. Do not plunder your neighbor's house or steal the goods of one that is near you, lest he denounce you before you are even heard. One who is argumentative is a mildless person. If he is also known as an aggressor, then that hostile man will have trouble in the neighborhood.

32. Be circumspect in matters of sexual relations.

33. If you examine the character of a friend, don't ask other people, approach your friend. Deal with him alone, so as not to suffer from his anger. You may argue with him after a little while. You may test his heart in conversation. If what he has seen escapes him, if he does something that annoys you, stay friendly with him and do not attack. Be restrained and don't answer him with hostility. Do not leave him and do not attack him. His time will not fail to come. He cannot escape his fate.

34. Be generous as long as you live. What leaves the storehouse does not return. It is the food in the storehouse that one must

share that is coveted. One whose belly is empty becomes an accuser. One who is deprived becomes an opponent. Therefore, do not have an accuser or an opponent as a neighbor. Your kindness to your neighbors will be a memorial to you for years, after you satisfy their needs.

35. Know your friends and then you prosper. Don't be mean towards your friends. They are like a watered field and greater than any material riches that you may have, for what belongs to one belongs to another. The character of one who is well born should be a profit to him. Good nature is a memorial.

36. Punish firmly and chastise soundly, then repression of crime becomes an example. But punishment except for crime will turn the complainer into an enemy.

37. If you take for a wife a good time woman who is joyful and who is well known in the town, if she is fickle and seems to live for the moment, do not reject her. Let her eat. The joyful person brings happiness.

If you listen to my saying all of your affairs will go forward. Their value resides in their truth. The memory of these sayings goes on in the speech of men and women because of the worth of their precepts. If every word is carried on, they will not perish in this land. If advice is given for the good, the great will speak accordingly. This is a matter of teaching a person to speak to posterity. He or she who hears it becomes a master hearer. It is good to speak to posterity. Posterity will listen.

If an example is set by him or her who leads, he or she will be beneficent forever, his wisdom lasting for all time. The wise person feeds the Ka with what endures, so that it is happy with that person on earth. The wise is known by his good actions. The heart of the wise matches his or her tongue and his or her lips are straight when he or she speaks. The wise have eyes that are made to see and ears that are made to hear what will profit the offspring. The wise person who acts with Maat is free of falsehood and disorder.

Useful is hearing to a son who hears. If hearing enters the hearer, then the hearer becomes a listener. Hearing well is speaking well. Useful is hearing to one who hears. Hearing is better than every thing else. It creates good will. How good it is for a son to understand his father's words. That son will reach old age through those words.

He who hears is beloved of God. He whom God hates does not hear. The heart makes of its owner a hearer or a non-hearer. Man's heart is his life, prosperity and health. The hearer is one who hears what is said. He who loves to hear is one who acts on what is said. How good it is for a son to listen to his father. How happy is he to whom it is said "Your son, is a master of hearing." The hearer of whom this is said is well endowed indeed and is honored by his father. That hearer's remembrance is in the mouth of the living, those that are on earth and those who will be.

If a man's son accepts his father's words then no plan of his will go wrong. So teach your son to be a hearer, one who will be valued by the officials, one who will guide his speech by what he has been told, one who is regarded as a hearer. This son will excel and his deeds will stand out while failure will follow those who do not hear. The wise wakes up early to his lasting gain while the fool is hard pressed.

The fool who does not hear, he can do nothing at all. He looks at ignorance and sees knowledge. He looks at harmfulness and sees usefulness. He does everything that one detests and is blamed for it every day. He lives on the things by which one dies. His food is evil speech.

His sort is known to the officials who say, "There goes a living death every day." One ignores the things that he does because of his many daily troubles.

A son who hears is a follower of Heru. When he is old and has reached the period where he is venerated, then he will speak likewise to his own children, renewing then the teachings of his father.

Every man teaches as he acts. He will speak to the children so that they will speak to their children. He will set an example and not give offense. So if justice stands firm, your children will live. As to the first child who gets into trouble, when people see it, they will say about the child "that is just like him", and they will also say when they even hear a rumor about the child, "that is just like him too."

To see everyone is to satisfy the many. Any riches that you have are useless without the many. Don't say something and then take it back. Don't put one thing in place of another. Beware of releasing the restraints in you, least the wise man say, "listen, if you want to endure in the mouth of the hearers, speak after you have mastered the craft." If you speak to good purpose all your affairs will be in place.

Conceal your heart. Control your mouth. Then you will be known among the officials. Be quite exact before your leader. Act so that no one wil! say to him "he is the son of that one."

Be deliberate when you speak so as to say things that count. Then the officials who listen will say, "how good is the thing that comes from his mouth." Act so that your leader will say of you, "how good is he whom his father has taught. When he came forth from his body, he told him all that was in his mind, and he does even more than he was told."

The good son is the gift of God and exceeds what is told him by his leader. He will do right when his heart is straight. As you succeed me sound in body, a Pharaoh, content with all that was done, may you obtain many years of life.

The things that I did on earth were not small. I have had 110 years of life. As a gift of the Pharaoh, I have had honors exceeding those of the ancestors, by doing Maat until the state of veneration.

It is done, from its beginning to its end, as it was found in the writings of the ancestors and Deity.

POSTSCRIPT

A counselor who understands proverbs soon sets difficult matters aright.

African Proverb

The Teachings of Ptahhotep are important for many reasons. We may note among those reasons, that they provide us with but a mere glimpse of a profoundly intellectual and spiritual body of thought and way of life of Africa's ancient people. Ptahhotep himself appeals to the Ancients, so ancient in fact that they were said to have been instructed by the Gods. Ptahhotep therefore laid no claim to original authorship. His wisdom was that of his people and of the Deity. Imagine what it would be like to have the whole papyrus that was found by Prisse. Imagine even more how it would be to have the whole body of literature of which the Teachings of this one priest were but a small fragment. It is through developed culture that we know who these ancient Africans were.

Compare the Ptahhotep fragments of African wisdom teachings to the Mesopotamian Code developed many centuries later by Hammurabi. For example, in Hammurabi, we may find a toleration for slavery, if not a wholesale justification for it. Compare also the role of leader in Ptahhotep with that described millennia later in Europe by Machiavelli in the "Prince." Machiavelli's prince was an unprincipled demagog, a true totalitarian. By contrast, Ptahhotep and other scribe priests taught a supremely democratic and humane system of thought.

The study of this sacred text and of all the other ancient Kemetic sacred texts is essential to an understanding both of Africa and of the development of world and "western civilization." It takes no major effort to see in these and other ancient Kemetic texts the antecedents to Biblical literature, to "Greek philosophy," and to eastern religions as well.

Cheikh Anta Diop, E.A. Wallis Budge, and many other scholars who knew both general African culture and that of Africa's most well known nation, KMT, were clear and confident about the unity of cultural forms between KMT and its sister nations of Africa. Therefore, these teachings do not merely illuminate the mind of Ptahhotep or Kemetic ways of life. They illuminate general African culture, from ancient times to the present.

Because we now have the actual words of Ancient Africa available to us today, we can understand better the hysterical attack of Roman politicians and some of the early Christian church fathers who ordered the closing of the Ancient Egyptian University or "mysteries system," the world's original system of higher education. What is "pagan", "animistic", "heathenish" or "barbarian", about Ptahhotep? Why were his and other writings ordered destroyed? Clearly the restoration of these writings destroys forever the myth of Africa that was created by greedy colonizers to justify their wanton destruction of African cultural competitors, the capture of their national wealth and the theft of their intellectual legacy as well.

Through the use of indigenous African literature, African people worldwide have the information to counter attempts to make us feel inferior by ruling us out of human history. Further, our own cultural traditions provide ample answers to the basic human questions that all must ask. We can start from our own African center in the creation of a future. Finally, we can once again share this humane, democratic, and deeply spiritual way of life with the world.

Africa continues to teach! May Amun be satisfied.

I have tried to bring out the profound cultural unity still alive beneath the deceptive appearance of cultural heterogeneity... Only a real knowledge of the past can keep in one's consciousness the feeling of historical continuity essential to the consolidation of a multinational state.

Cheikh Anta Diop

SELECTED BIBLIOGRAPHY

Baines, J. (1983). "Literacy And Ancient Egyptian Society," Man, N.S., 18, pp. 572-99.

Baker, William H. (1917). West African Folktales. London: Harrap.

Battiscombe, G. Gunn. (1909). The Instruction of Ptahhotep. London.

Ben Jochannan, Yosef. (1974). The Black Man's Religion And Extracts And Comments From The Holy Black Bible. New York: Alkebulan Books Associates.

Ben Jochannan, Yosef. (1978). Our "Black Seminarians" And " Black Clergy": Without A " Black Theology". New York: Alkebulan Books And Education Materials Associates.

Breasted, James Henry. (1912). A History Of Egypt: From The Earliest Times To The Persian Conquest. New York: Charles Scribners And Sons.

Cardinal, Allan W. (1931). Tales Told In Togoland, London: Oxford University Press.

Carruthers, Jacob H. (1984). Essays In Ancient Egyptian Studies, Los Angeles: Timbuktu Publishers.

d'avennes, E. Prisse. (1858). Fac-simile d'un papyrus egyptien en caracteres hieratiques, Trouve a Thebes, donne a la Bibliotheque Royale de Paris, et publie par E. Prisse d'avennes. Paris: Imprimerie Lithographique de Lemercier.

Edwards, Amelia B. (1892). Pharoahs, Fellahs And Explorers. New York.

Erman, Adolf. (1927). The Literature Of The Ancient Egyptians, London: Methuen.

Frankfort, et al. (1977). The Intellectual Adventure Of Ancient Man: An Essay On Speculative Thought In The Ancient Near East, Chicago: University Of Chicago Press.

Griaule, Marcel And Dieterlen, Germaine. (1986). The Pale Fox. Arizona: Continuum Foundation.

Heath,. (1856). "On A manuscript Of The Phoenician King Assa, ruling in Egypt earlier than Abraham; A Record of the patriarchal Age; or, The Proverbs Of Aphobis, B.C. 1900;" Monthly Review, London, July.

Jackson, John G. (1980). The Mysteries Of Egypt. Chicago: Mass, Inc.

James, George G.M. (1976). Stolen Legacy. San Francisco: Julian Richardson Associates.

Karenga, Maulana. (1984). Selections From The Husia: Scared Wisdom Of Ancient Egypt. Los Angeles:

University Of Sankore Press

Karenga, Maulana And Carruthers, Jacob H. (1986). Kemet And The African Worldview: Research Rescue And Restoration. Los Angeles: University Of Sankore Press

Kuhn, Alvin Boyd. (1949). Shadow Of The Third Century: Revaluation Of Christianity, New Jersey: Academy Press.

Lamy, Lucie. (1981). Egyptian Mysteries: New Light On Ancient Spiritual Knowledge, New York: Crossroads Publishers.

Lesko, Leonard H. (1972). The Ancient Egyptian Book Of Two Ways, Berkeley: University Of California Press.

Lichtheim, Miriam. (1980). Ancient Egyptian Literature, 3 vols, Berkeley: University Of California Press.

Mayer, Josephine and Prideaux, Tom. (1938). Never To Die: The Egyptians In Their Own Words, New York.

Montet, Pierre. (1964). Eternal Egypt, New York: The New American Library.

Murray, Margaret A. (1972). The Splendour That Was Egypt, London.

Myer, Isaac. (1900). Oldest Books In The World: An Account Of The Religion, Wisdom, Philosophy, Ethics, Psychology, Manners, Proverbs, Sayings And Refinement, etc. New York: E.W. Dayton.

Nobles, Wade W. (1984). "Ancient Egyptian Thought And The Development Of Afrikan (Black) Psychology." Presented to the First Annual Ancient Egyptian Studies Conference, Los Angeles, Feb. 24-26.

Oesterley, W.O.E. (1927). The Wisdom Of Egypt In The Old Testament, London: The African Publication Society.

Olela, Henry. (1981). From Ancient Africa To Ancient Greece: An Introduction To The history Of Philosophy, Atlanta: Black Heritage Corporation and Select Publishing Corp.

Peet, T. Eric. (1931). A Comparative Study Of The Literature Of Egypt, Palestine And Mesopotamia, London: Oxford university Press.

Rattray, Robert S. (1916). Ashanti Proverbs. Oxford.

Rattray, Robert S. (1913). Hausa Folklore. Oxford: Clarendon Press.

Save-Soderbergh, Torgny. (1961) Pharoahs And Mortals. London: Robert hale Limited.

Schure, Edouard. (1977). The Great Initiates: A Study Of The Secret History Of Religions. New York: Multimedia Publishing Co.

Schwaller de Lubicz, Isha. (1978). Her-Bak: The Egyptian Initiate. London.

Schwaller de Lubicz, R.A. (1978). Symbol And The Symbolic. Mass.: Autumn Press.

Schwaller de Lubicz, R.A. (1985). The Egyptian Miracle: An Introduction To The Wisdom Of The Temple. New York: Transactions.

Simpson, William K. (ed.) (1972). The Literature Of Ancient Egypt. New York: Yale University Press.

Van Sertima, Ivan. (1985). Nile Valley Civilizations: Proceedings Of The Nile Valley Conference. Alanta, Georgia: Sept. 26-30. Journal Of African Civilizations, New York: Transactions.

West, John Anthony. (1979). Serpent In The Sky: The High Wisdom Of Ancient Egypt. New York: Harper And Row.

Weigall, Arthur. (1928). Personalities Of Antiquity. New York: Doubleday.

Williams, Chancellor. (1961). The Rebirth Of African Civilization. Washington: Public Affairs Press.

Woodson, Carter G., (1928). <u>African Myths</u>. Washington, D.C.: Associated Publishers.

KEMETIC GLOSSARY

Amun - The hidden one, shown with a tall crown of feathers; often also in the form of Min. from 2000 to 1360 B.C. he is pre-eminent among Kemetic deities.

Dynasty - A succession of rulers of the same line of descent Thirty dynasties of Kemetic Kings were listed by the priest Manetho, from Menes to Ptolemy II Philadelphus.

Hapi - God or neter of the Nile, self-engendered; lord of the fish represented by an androgynous divinity crowned by a papyrus reed.

Horus/Heru - Prehistoric Kemetic sky god in the form of a falcon Horus was said to be the parthenogenetic child of the Virgin Mother Isis. In the catacombs of Rome, black statues of this Kemetic divine Mother and Infant still survive from the early Christian worship of the Virgin and Child to which they were converted.

Kamite - the name used by the indigenous inhabitants of the region of upper and lower Kemet to refer to themselves.

Kemet (KMT) - the black land; the ancient name of Ancient Egypt.

Ka - the double of a living person in Ancient Kemet. The "double" was an integral part of man, and was connected with his shadow, and came into being when he was born, and lived in the tomb with the body after death.

Khufu - builder of the Great Pyramid at Giza.

Luxor - The center of government during the 18th dynasty of Kemet. It was named Wa-Set meaning "The Septer." It was part of the ancient site of Thebes. A huge temple dedicated to the god Amun was built in the reign of Amenhotep III and altered by succeeding Pharoahs. This was the largest temple of ancient times, the Ipet Isut, called karnak by the Arabs. These magnificent buildings existed long before there was a Greece, and even longer before Greeks would conquer KMT under Alexander the Great. Ipet Isut meant "the most select of places," or "the holiest of places." It was both a center of religion and education. It housed an elite faculty of priest-professors. It has been estimated that at one time there were more than 80,000 students at all grade levels studying at Ipet Isut University.

Maat - truth, justice, righteousness, balance, order. The personification of order of the world which was established at creation; shown as a woman with a feather in her hair. She was considered to be the daughter of the creator god (Re), had a widespread cult, and is also found doubled as the "two Maats" from an early period.

Manetho - Kemetic Priest in the reign of Ptolemy I who wrote a history of Kemet in Greek. His division of Kings of Kemet into 30 dynasties is still used in Egyptian history.

Mdw Ntr (Mdw Netcher) - Sacred Writing; the Greeks called this first writing system of the world "hieroglyphics." This ancient system of writing was decoded by Jean Francois Champollion after deciphering the Rosetta Stone. The African-American Norbert Rillieux (sugar refinery) worked closely with Champollion on the project.

Middle Kingdom - (2050 - 1786 B.C.); Ancient Egypt's Middle Kingdom must be regarded as one of the most remarkable epochs in the long history of African people. From 2050 - 1786 B.C., the Middle Kingdom contributed some of Africa's most significant literary and religious innovations. Its literature set the standard of future generations. Its art was held in such esteem that it was used as a model in the Egyptian renaissance of the last native dynasties. In the fields of scientific and technical proficiency, the Blacks took giant steps and left a record of genius that continues to amaze modern scholars. Its colossal, yet precise, construction projects have few parallels, past or present. Of its Kings, several were giants, whose worship was preserved intact for more than a thousand years. Also of note, a fact of supreme importance — the civilization of Egypt's Middle Kingdom was a product of neither Europe nor Asia — but the Upper Nile Valley, towards the interior of Africa (Rashidi, 1983).

New Kingdom - Covers 18th and 19th dynasties, 1580 1350 B.C. and 1350 - 1200 B.C. The Hyksos invaders were crushed and a military state embarked on wide conquest from as far as Cush to the Euphrates.

Nile River - longest river in the world 4145 miles long flowing in Africa.

Nubia - The Narrow Valley of the Nile River south of Aswan as far as the second Cataract region in the Sudan.

Osiris/Asar - King of the Underworld and Lord of the Dead. his wife was Isis and his sons included Heru and Anubis. he most frequently appears in mummy form.

Papyrus - The name of Kemetic Kings and synonymous with kingship. It derives from the Kemetic term per-aa or "Great house"' meaning the palace of the King.

Ptahhotep - A Vizier of the Old Kingdom credited with having set down celebrated precepts of morality and ethics.

Sakkara - situated 28 Kilometers south of modern Cairo, just west of Memphis and south of Giza. Ancient burial site named after Sokar, the god of measure. Graves dated from the 1st dynasty. Pyramids attributed to the 5th and 6th dynasties. Site of the step pyramid of Imhotep of the 3rd dynasty.

Seneferu - (2700 B.C.), First King of the fourth Dynasty. Father of Khufu. Built bent pyramid at Medum.

Step Pyramid - the oldest stone building in the world, built by Imhotep for King Zoser at Sakkara.

Ta Seti - land of the bow, site of the world's first monarchy in Nubia at Qustul.

Thebes/Waset - Capital of Ancient Egypt. During the New Kingdom it was the center of Egypt's empire. The modern city of Luxor is on the site of the Ancient Metropolis.

Vizier - This was an important office in Kemet. He was the Pharoah's Prime Minister and was responsible for running the Kingdom. He had to travel about from district to district and see that all was going smoothly and that the local officials were carrying out their tasks.

BIOGRAPHICAL NOTES ON EDITORS

Nia Damali

Nia Damali was born in Chicago, Illinois. She received her B.A. from Clark College in Atlanta, Georgia, and she's presently working toward a Master's Degree. She is the author of three books including "Poetry of My Identity", "I Am Natural", and "Golden Names For An African People". Her work has appeared in magazines and journals such as Black American Literature Forum, Network Africa, The New York Quarterly, Catalyst, The Black Nation, and others. She has traveled and studied extensively in Kenya and Egypt where she has gathered source materials for various writing projects. She has written several plays and short stories and has performed throughout Chicago and the Atlanta, area.

Asa G. Hilliard III

Asa G. Hilliard III is an educational psychologist and is a distinguished Professor of Education at Georgia State University. He served previously as Dean of the School of Education at San Francisco State University.

In addition to his work as an educational psychologist, Dr. Hilliard has specialized in the study of Ancient African Civilizations, especially Ancient Kemet. Dr. Hilliard has conducted a number of study tours to Egypt. he has also contributed articles on Kemet to scholarly journals, such as Journal Of African Civilizations. Recently he completed a thirteen part television series for South Carolina Educational Television. In this series "Free Your Mind Return To The Source: African Origins," Dr. Hilliard presents parts of his classic slide lecture on the documentation of ancient African History.

Dr. Hilliard has published widely on many topics. He is co-author with Dr. Barbara Sizemore and others of Saving The African American Child. A Report of the National Alliance of Black School Educators.

Larry Williams

Larry Williams has had wide experience in the field of African and African-American Studies, as a historian, researcher and lecturer. He has been instrumental in organizing numerous conferences such as, The Return To The Source Conference 1983, The Nile Valley Conference 1984 and the Southern Regional Kemetic Studies Conference 1986. As a historian he has been published in the <u>Journal of African Civilizations, History, the Bible And Black Man Magazine, Return to the Source Magazine</u>, the <u>Atlanta Voice Newspaper</u> and <u>Afrika Must Unite: A Journal or Pan-African Affairs</u>. he was a contributing author in the Black studies teachers guide titled, <u>From Ancient Africa To African-Americans Today</u> for the Portland Public Schools. Mr. Williams is the Co-Editor of the Journal of African Civilizations special issue, <u>GREAT AFRICAN THINKERS, Vol. I: Cheikh Anta Diop</u>.